For David Huffman
with thanks for twenty-five years
of vigorous Christian friendship

WORLDVIEW GUIDE

The ILIAD

Dr. Louis Markos

canonpress
Moscow, Idaho

Published by Canon Press
P.O. Box 8729, Moscow, Idaho 83843
800.488.2034 | www.canonpress.com

Dr. Louis Markos, *Worldview Guide for the Iliad*
Copyright © 2019 by Louis Markos.
For the Canon Classics edition of the epic (2017), go to www.canonpress.
com/books/canon-classics.

Cover design by James Engerbretson
Cover illustrations by Forrest Dickison
Interior design by Valerie Anne Bost and James Engerbretson

Printed in the United States of America.

Library of Congress Cataloging-in-Publication Data:
Markos, Louis, author.
Iliad worldview guide / Louis Markos.
Moscow, Idaho : Canon Press, 2019.
LCCN 2019011333 | ISBN 9781944503901 (pbk. : alk. paper)
LCSH: Homer. Iliad.
Classification: LCC PA4037 .M3237 2019 | DDC 883/.01--dc23
LC record available at https://lccn.loc.gov/2019011333

A free end-of-book test and answer key are available for download at
www.canonpress.com/ClassicsQuizzes

17 18 19 20 21 22   9 8 7 6 5 4 3 2 1

CONTENTS

INTRODUCTION

It is no exaggeration to say that every western and war movie ever made owes a debt to Homer's *Iliad*. All that man has thought or said about the glory and horror of the battlefield, the internal struggle of the soldier, and the inescapable nature of our mortality is contained within the pages of Homer's epic. It is here that western literature begins, here that the big questions begin to be asked, here that beauty meets truth.

THE WORLD AROUND

There was almost surely a real war fought between the Greeks and the Trojans, whose city of Troy was located on the northwest coast of modern day Turkey. And that war was most likely fought around 1200 BC, at the height of the Mycenaean Bronze Age.

When we speak of the Mycenaeans, we speak of a loosely federated group of individual city-states spread out across Greece, but mostly located in the Peloponnese. The chief of these city-states was Mycenae, but there were others at Argos, Sparta, Pylos, Salamis, Phthia, Thebes, and Athens, not to mention the islands of Crete and Ithaca. The leader of each city-state was a king in his own right, though they all looked to Agamemnon of Mycenae as their commander-in-chief.[1]

---

1. For a fascinating and accessible introduction to Homer and his world, see Michael Wood's *In Search of the Trojan War* (Berkeley: University of California, 1998). This is based on Wood's own excellent PBS series.

Although the Mycenaeans defeated the Trojans, they did not set up any bases in Troy; instead, they returned home with their plunder. But their glory and power was not to last much longer. By 1100, Mycenaean civilization had collapsed, plunging Greece into a three-hundred-year Dark Age during which the art of writing was lost.

In the absence of writing, an oral tradition sprang up to preserve the memory of the Golden Age of Mycenae. That oral tradition was later carried across the Aegean to the coast of modern-day Turkey, where it was systematized and perfected by a group of bards who learned the skill of reciting long tales from memory.

Homer was the last in a long line of bards. He did not invent the *Iliad*, but constructed it from the oral tradition that had been passed down to him.

ABOUT THE AUTHOR

Though Homer was a Greek, he did not live in Greece but somewhere along the Asia Minor coast (modern-day Turkey). Seven cities competed for his birthplace, but he was most likely a resident of the island of Chios. Though we do not know for certain if Homer was blind, there is good reason to believe that he was—especially given the fact that he includes a blind bard in the *Odyssey* who may very well be a surrogate for himself.

The genius of Homer did not consist in his ability to "make up" stories out of his imagination, but to give shape to tales that had been handed down to him in a fragmented form. It was most likely Homer who chose to center the *Iliad* on the character of Achilles rather than, say, Agamemnon or Ajax or Diomedes. He also found creative ways to connect separate episodes both dramatically and thematically.

Though he most likely lived near the end of the eighth century BC, at a time when Greece was reclaiming her

written language from the Phoenicians, Homer was almost surely illiterate. The excessive use of repetition and
"descriptive epithets" clearly identifies the epic as a prod-
uct of oral composition.

If Homer did indeed compose both the *Iliad* and *Odyssey*, and the full weight of ancient tradition says that he
did, then he truly belongs in the category of Shakespeare.
Whereas most great writers specialize in one specific
genre and one defining mood, Homer, like Shakespeare,
was equally adept at presenting tragedy (*Iliad*) and come-
dy (*Odyssey*) and at celebrating both war and peace, death
and marriage.

WHAT OTHER
NOTABLES SAID

It would be difficult to find a critic who did not have something positive to say about the *Iliad* of Homer. Western literature begins with the *Iliad*, and almost everything that has come after it has been influenced in some way by it.

And yet, the first great literary critic, Plato, kicked Homer and his poetic heirs out of his perfect republic because Plato felt that Homer's poetry led people farther away from the truth about gods, men, and the universe. In the opening of Book X of the *Republic*, Plato, through the guise of Socrates, confesses, "I have always from my earliest youth had an awe and love of Homer which even now makes the words falter on my lips, for he seems to be the great captain and teacher of the whole of that noble tragic company; but a man is not to be reverenced more than the truth, and therefore I will speak out."[2]

---

2. Plato, *The Republic*, in *Critical Theory Since Plato*, rev. edition, ed. by Hazard Adams (New York: HBJ, 1992), 31.

Plato's famous (or infamous) critique of poetry as being an imitation of an imitation of the truth has certainly had much influence over the last 2,500 years, but, luckily for lovers of poetry, his critique was answered soon after by his star pupil, Aristotle. In his *Poetics*, Aristotle offers a positive view of poetic imitation as a process that brings us *closer* to the truth. In chapter nine, Aristotle celebrates the author of the *Iliad* by saying that "in the serious style, Homer is preeminent among poets, for he alone combined narrative form with excellence of imitation."[3]

Nearly all future critics of Homer have followed Aristotle rather than Plato, agreeing with the ancient critic Longinus that Homer's *Iliad* embodies to perfection a quality which he called the sublime and which he defined as "the echo of a great soul." In fact, Longinus went so far as to argue that Plato reached sublimity in his philosophy only because "he had with all his soul and mind struggled with Homer for the primacy."[4]

---

3. Aristotle, *The Poetics*, in *Critical Theory*, 52.

4. Longinus, *On the Sublime*, in *Critical Theory*, 79, 84.

SETTING, CHARACTERS, AND PLOT SUMMARY

- *Setting: The city of Troy (northwest coast of Turkey) near the end of the 13th century BC*
- *Agamemnon:* Son of Atreus, King of Mycenae, Commander-in-Chief of the Greek army
- *Menelaus:* Brother of Agamemnon, King of Sparta, husband of Helen
- *Achilles:* King of Phthia and greatest warrior of the Greeks
- *Patroclus:* Best friend of Achilles
- *Odysseus:* King of Ithaca and most clever of the Greek soldiers
- *Ajax* (also known as *Aias*): Second strongest Greek soldier after Achilles
- *Diomedes:* Third strongest Greek soldier after Achilles and Ajax
- *Nestor:* King of Pylos who, though too old to fight, acts as an advisor to Agamemnon

- *Helen:* Wife of Menelaus, brought to Troy by Paris; her kidnapping started the Trojan War
- *Chryseis:* Captive woman of Agamemnon whom he is forced to return
- *Briseis:* Captive woman of Achilles whom Agamemnon takes
- *Priam:* King of Troy, husband of Hecuba, father of Hector and Paris
- *Hector:* Prince of Troy and greatest Trojan warrior; husband of Andromache
- *Paris:* Brother of Hector who steals away Helen and starts the Trojan War
- *Zeus:* King of the gods, husband and brother of Hera, promises to help Achilles
- *Hera:* Queen of the gods who favors the Greeks and hates Paris and the Trojans
- *Thetis:* Minor sea goddess who marries the mortal Peleus and bears Achilles
- *Apollo:* Son of Zeus and brother of Artemis who favors Trojans over Greeks
- *Hephaestus:* Blacksmith of the gods who makes new armor for Achilles

The *Iliad* does not begin at the beginning of the Trojan War but chronicles a period of less than two weeks in the final year of a long and grueling ten-year war. Because of Troy's massive walls, the Greeks prove unable to defeat their enemy and are forced to raid nearby cities for supplies. After raiding the city of Thebe, Agamemnon takes the best prize for himself, the lovely Chryseis, even though Achilles fought the hardest and best.

Shortly after the raid, a plague strikes the Greek camp. Achilles calls a soothsayer (Calchas) to divulge the origin of the plague. When Calchas reveals that the plague can only be ended if Agamemnon returns Chryseis to her father, a priest of Apollo, Agamemnon refuses. The hotheaded Achilles challenges him and a war of words breaks out that ends with Agamemnon stealing away Achilles' war prize (Briseis) in compensation for having to surrender his own. In response, Achilles pulls out of the war and asks his goddess mother (Thetis) to pray to Zeus to avenge him.

In answer to Thetis' prayer, Zeus allows the Trojans to gain the upper hand, forcing Agamemnon to swallow his pride and beg Achilles to return to the battlefield. However, although Agamemnon offers Achilles a veritable treasure trove if he will return, the still-angry soldier refuses. Without Achilles, the Greeks are overrun by the Trojans, who are led by Hector, son of Priam.

Finally, desperate to help the Greeks, Achilles' friend Patroclus begs to wear Achilles' armor and lead Achilles' troops into battle. Achilles agrees, but warns Patroclus not to take on Hector by himself. Sadly, Patroclus, caught up in the fever of battle, ignores Achilles' advice and is killed by Hector, who strips him of Achilles' armor and wears it himself.

Enraged, Achilles reenters the battle, swearing that he will kill Hector or die himself. With new armor forged for him by Hephaestus, Achilles mows down the Trojan army until, at last, he comes face to face with Hector, who initially runs away from the furious Achilles but then turns and faces him. Achilles kills him, strips off his armor, and drags his naked body around the walls of Troy while Hector's family looks on from the wall.

When it becomes clear that Achilles' rage and grief will never end, Zeus intervenes and helps Priam to sneak into the Greek camp to ransom the dead body of his son from Achilles. Achilles honors the plea of the broken Priam and the two weep together in a moment of shared humanity. Though the original audience of the *Iliad* knew that the Greeks would soon defeat Troy (by means of the notorious Trojan Horse) and raze the city to the ground, Homer chose to end his bloody epic with a lull in the war during which Hector is given a glorious funeral.

WORLDVIEW ANALYSIS

It is a given, or at least *should* be a given, of the Christian worldview that human nature does not change. We are not simply products of our socioeconomic milieu, as the Marxists would have it, nor of dark subconscious forces over which we have no ultimate control, as the Freudians would have it. We are, rather, creatures who were made in God's image but are fallen. Whatever age or culture into which we have been born, we bear that dual mark of glory and depravity.

If we pay careful attention as we read Book I of the *Iliad*, we will recognize the struggle between Achilles and Agamemnon, not because we are projecting our own cultural baggage onto Homer's epic, but because we share a common humanity with Achilles, Agamemnon, and Homer. In a nutshell, the quarrel that breaks out between the commander-in-chief of the combined Greek forces and the greatest of warriors is the age-old struggle between the politician and the soldier, the administrator and the teacher, the high priest and the prophet.

The first person in each of these pairs is the bureaucrat who must maintain law and order, while the second is the charismatic loner who has little regard for the rules. The former feels threatened by the latter, while the latter feels underappreciated by the former. Think of the relationship between the paranoid King Saul and the popular David in 1 Samuel, or the suspicious, ethnocentric leaders of the Jerusalem church and the newly-converted, iconoclastic Saul of Tarsus in Acts.

If we are to grow as Christians and as human beings, we must understand the nature of this struggle, and thus of our own capacity for self-destruction. We must seek out moderation when our passions would tear us apart out of fear or rage, suspicion or egocentrism. There is a wealth of wisdom in James's admonition to "be quick to hear, slow to speak, slow to anger" (James 1:19; ESV).

In the episode in Book I, Nestor, empowered by the proverbial wisdom of experience, is able temporarily to calm down Agamemnon and Achilles, but the two antagonists nevertheless set in motion the actions that will lead to tragedy. Desperate to save face before his men and to show the younger Achilles he is not afraid of him, Agamemnon unjustly steals away Achilles' prize. His ego wounded, Achilles pulls out of the war and utters the prayer that will bring death to his fellow Greeks . . . and to his best friend. None of us lives in a vacuum; our decisions have far wider consequences than we can imagine.

* * * * *

Like the Bible itself, the *Iliad* refuses to give us easy, black-and-white situations. Though we are clearly on the side of the Greeks, Homer presents the Trojans in a positive light. Priam and Hecuba are a good and honorable king and queen ruling over a civilized, family-centered city. Prince Hector and his wife, Andromache, are a mature and loving couple for whom all readers feel immediate sympathy. Indeed, when Hector says farewell to Andromache in the final scene of Book VI, Homer captures for all time the essence of the husband/wife, masculine/feminine relationship celebrated in Genesis 2.

Rather than brush off Andromache's request that he remain within the walls of Troy and let others fight on the battlefield, Hector gently and compassionately explains to her why he cannot do that. Hector was raised from childhood "to fight always in the foremost ranks of the Trojans, / winning for my own self great glory, and for my father" (VI.445-446).[5] Hector is not an autonomous individual motivated only by self-interest. He exists within a web of relationships that define him as a man, a son, a prince, a husband, a father, and a general. Modern readers

---

5. All quotes from Homer are taken from *The Iliad of Homer*, translated by Richmond Lattimore (Chicago: University of Chicago, 1951). References are given by book and line number.

of this moving scene, which was written by a pagan poet some seven centuries before the birth of Christ, will find themselves drawn toward a model of the family and the human person that is, in many ways, more biblical than that found in the works of many a twenty-first century Christian writer. We pat ourselves on the back for having "liberated" women, yet the tenderness with which Hector responds to Andromache surpasses that of most husbands today. Responding to his wife's fears, Hector explains to her that he will die on the day that fate has appointed, whether or not he remains home or returns to the battle-field. Since he cannot escape his fate, let him at least be true to his calling.

He then comforts her with a complementarian vision of marriage that our modern age is quickly losing. According to that vision, he must labor to fulfill the work of his sphere while she must labor to fulfill her own: "Go therefore back to our house, and take up your own work, / the loom and the distaff, and see to it that your hand-maidens / ply their work also; but the men must see to the fighting, / all men who are the people of Ilion, but I beyond others" (VI.486-93). As long as the two of them take up their separate spheres, he embodying courage and devotion to duty and she embodying the virtues of the wife described so eloquently in Proverbs 31, all will be well, and they will be able to find stability in a world that is tearing itself apart.

* * * * *

If Hector is a man who stays true to the code of his culture, then Achilles is something at once nobler and more terrifying. While Hector embraces his fate and his impending death, Achilles rages against his own mortality. Most readers of the *Iliad* come to the epic knowing an ancient story about Achilles—that his body, with the exception of his heel, is impervious to all weapons. This is because his goddess mother, Thetis, held him by the heel and dipped him in the river Styx when he was a baby.

Everyone knows this story, and yet Homer refuses to tell it. His hero is not the greatest warrior who ever took the field because he has superhuman skin, but because his life is devoted to battle. Achilles knows only fighting and war; he does not fear pain or flinch when the battle is at its height. However, as a close reading of the *Iliad* makes clear, he is morbidly obsessed with his own death. The reason for this is quite simple. Since he was a child, his immortal mother has been bemoaning the fact that her mortal son will die young and leave her to grieve alone.

Of course, Achilles' mortality makes him one with every person who has ever read the *Iliad*. When our first parents, Adam and Eve, ate of the forbidden fruit (Gen. 3), they ushered death into the world; since that fateful day, every human being has had to wrestle with the inescapability of his impending mortality. From the moment of our birth, we are moving inexorably toward our death. We can rage against it, we can try all means to prevent it, but we will succumb in the end to the power of death.

Before pulling out of the war in Book I, Achilles compensates for his mortality in the same way that all his fellow soldiers do: by gathering up as many war trophies—or "meeds of honor"—as he can, thus achieving a sort of surrogate immortality. But after he refuses to fight any longer and is forced to look on from the sidelines, he begins to reexamine his attachment to war prizes (such as Briseis, whom Agamemnon steals from him in Book I). That Achilles *has* been reexamining the link between meeds of honor and immortality is made clear in Book IX, when Agamemnon sends a delegation of three carefully-chosen men—the smooth-tongued Odysseus to woo the recalcitrant Achilles, the killing-machine Ajax to appeal to his bloodlust, and his former tutor, Phoinix, to inject a personal touch—to urge Achilles to return to battle and save the Greeks.

The men do not come empty-handed. Through them, Agamemnon promises to give Achilles more meeds of honor than any soldier has ever received, thus ensuring Achilles' immortality as the greatest and most honorable warrior in Greek history. But Achilles, to everyone's shock and surprise, refuses. Apart from any knowledge of God's revelation to the Jews, much less the later teachings of Socrates, Plato, and Aristotle, Achilles struggles his way toward an inchoate understanding that no one can put a price tag on a human life, for we are all born with inherent dignity and worth.

Thus, when his beloved tutor counsels him to take the meeds of honor offered him by Agamemnon, he replies,

"Phoinix my father, aged, illustrious, such honour is a thing / I need not. I think I am honoured already in Zeus' ordinance / which will hold me here beside my curved ships as long as life's wind / stays in my breast, as long as my knees have their spring beneath me" (IX.607-10). While this ethic would, I hope, sound like common sense to anyone who has grown up in a Judeo-Christian home, it is not an ethic honored by Homer's warriors. Ultimately, the only real source of the intrinsic value of each and every human life is the belief that we are all, rich and poor, brave and cowardly alike, made in the image of God.

* * * * *

Alas, Achilles' noble, proto-Christian ethic does not survive the death of Patroclus. To the contrary, when Patroclus dies, Achilles turns against his new ethic with bestial ferocity. It was that ethic, after all, that prevented Achilles from returning to battle and protecting Patroclus from the spear of Hector. Consumed by guilt, Achilles goes on the warpath, mowing down, without mercy, every soldier who comes into his path. His killing spree climaxes in a duel with Hector that ends with the latter's death.

Achilles thinks that once he exacts revenge on the killer of his friend, he will find peace, but that does not happen. Not content with killing Hector, Achilles strips him naked, ties ropes to his heels, and drags his corpse around and around the walls of Troy. Even that fails to assuage his grief. For ten days he jealously guards the corpse of Hector and continually defiles it. Taking pity on the dead hero, Apollo protects Hector's body from decay, but Achilles in his grief does not realize this. And so the defiling continues, while man and god alike stand silent before Achilles' unbalanced rage (which, incidentally, is the first word of the *Iliad* in the original Greek).

Though Achilles is only a single individual, his actions threaten to destroy the norms of pity and shame. Civilization is a balancing act at best; apart from a base of citizens who are morally self-regulating, who have God's law engraved in their hearts, it cannot withstand the kind of rage that is unleashed by Achilles. Homer's society lacks a single, holy God who can serve as a fixed, universal standard of moral-ethical behavior; at best, it survives by instilling honor codes in the hearts of such warrior-leaders as Hector and Achilles. What then, when the likes of Achilles reject such codes and embrace pitiless revenge?

Still, Homer *does* manage to bring about reconciliation in Book XXIV of the *Iliad*, a reconciliation that bears witness to the fact that though we are all sinners and cannot save ourselves, we yet retain the image of God. When it becomes clear that Achilles will not, on his own, let go of his revenge, Zeus has his son Hermes, the messenger of the gods, visit Priam and instruct him to sneak into the Greek camp and ransom back from Achilles the body of his son Hector.

In one of the tensest moments in all literature, Priam enters Achilles' tent and throws himself before the killer of his son. He begs Achilles to look upon him and take pity on his grief, to think of his own father and the grief he will feel when his son dies. Moved by Priam's courage, Achilles pities him and the two grieve together until their mutual sorrow, Priam for Hector and Achilles for Patroclus, passes for a time.

For most people, the hardest thing about being mortal is that it means we will someday die. In the final book of the *Iliad*, we learn, no matter our religious background, that what it really means to be mortal is that we will all lose someone whom we love. By sharing in their grief and thus affirming their shared mortality, Priam and Achilles rise above the horror and destruction of the Trojan War. The *Iliad* ends, not with the death of Achilles, which is prophesied in the epic, nor the fall of Troy, which will be brutal and total, but with a truce called by Greek and Trojan alike to allow them to bury their dead.

Homer composed his epic apart from any knowledge of the Bible, but he was a man made in God's image, and he succeeded in touching on the very core of our humanity. All people, but Christians in particular, can learn much of truth and value from Achilles' larger-than-life struggles with his mortality.

QUOTABLES

1. And the anger came upon Peleus' son, and within
   his shaggy breast the heart was divided two ways,
           pondering
   whether to draw from beside his thigh the sharp
           sword, driving
   away all those who stood between and kill the son
           of Atreus,
   or else to check the spleen within and keep down his anger.
   Now as he weighed in mind and spirit these two courses
   and was drawing from its scabbard the great sword,
           Athene descended . . .
   The goddess standing behind Peleus' son caught him by
           the fair hair,
   appearing to him only, for no man of the others saw her.[6]
                                ~ Book I.188–94, 197–98

---

6. All Quotables also from Lattimore's *Iliad*.

2.   So speaking glorious Hektor held out his arms to his baby,
     who shrank back to his fair-girdled nurse's bosom
     screaming, and frightened at the aspect of his own father,
     terrified as he saw the bronze and the crest with its
           horse-hair,
     nodding dreadfully, as he thought, from the peak of
           the helmet.
     Then his beloved father laughed out, and his honoured
           mother,
     and at once glorious Hektor lifted from his head the helmet
     and laid it in all its shining upon the ground. Then taking
     up his dear son he tossed him about in his arms, and
           kissed him . . .

     ~ Book VI.466–74

3.   "But now, seeing that the spirits of death stand close
           about us
     in their thousands, no man can turn aside nor escape them,
     let us go on and win glory for ourselves, or yield it to
           others."

     ~ *Homeric honor code,* Book XII.310–28

4.   "Hektor, argue me no agreements. I cannot forgive you.
     As there are no trustworthy oaths between men and lions,
     nor wolves and lambs have spirit that can be brought
           to agreement
     but forever these hold feelings of hate for each other,
     so there can be no love between you and me, nor shall
           there be
     oaths between us . . ."

     ~ *Achilles to Hector*, Book XXII.261–66

5. So [Priam] spoke, and stirred in the other a passion of
            grieving
    for his own father. He took the old man's hand and
            pushed him
    gently away, and the two remembered, as Priam sat huddled
    at the feet of Achilleus and wept close for man-
            slaughtering Hektor
    and Achilleus wept now for his own father, now again
    for Patroklos. The sound of their mourning moved in
            the house. Then
    when great Achilleus had taken full satisfaction in sorrow
    and the passion for it had gone from his mind
            and body . . .
    ~Achilles and Priam grieve together, Book XXIV.507–14

21 SIGNIFICANT QUESTIONS AND ANSWERS

1. What is the back story to the Trojan War?

    According to a myth that all of Homer's readers
    would have known but which is only briefly alluded
    to in the *Iliad*, the Trojan War began with the
    wedding of Achilles' parents, Thetis and Peleus. In
    revenge for not being invited to the party, Eris, the
    goddess of discord, tossed a golden apple into the
    party engraved with the words "to the fairest." Three
    goddesses, Hera, wife of Zeus, Athena, goddess of
    wisdom, and Aphrodite, goddess of love, all laid
    claim to the apple. When no god would choose,
    they convinced the mortal Paris to make the
    judgment. Swayed by Aphrodite's promise of the
    most beautiful girl in the world (Helen), he gave
    her the apple. Unfortunately, to get Helen, he had
    to steal her away from her husband, Menelaus, thus
    igniting the war between Greece (Menelaus was the

King of Sparta) and Troy (Paris was the Prince of
Troy).

2. Why does Homer choose to begin his epic in the final
    year of the Trojan War rather than with the beginning
    of the war?

    Rather than begin his epic *ab ovo* (Latin for "from
    the egg"), Homer plunges *in medias res* (Latin for
    "in the middle of things"), thus initiating an epic
    convention that is also used in most Greek trage-
    dies. (Other epic conventions include the invocation
    of the Muse, an opening proem that asks a ques-
    tion, catalogues of ships, place names, and warriors,
    extended descriptions of armor, funeral games, and
    the return of the hero.) By doing so, Homer is able
    to begin his epic at a moment of high tension and
    crisis and to tighten up the structure of what other-
    wise might be a loose, overly episodic narrative.

3. Why does the fight between Achilles and Agamemnon
    in Book I escalate so quickly?

    By beginning his epic *in medias res*, Homer can
    bank on there already being a history of conflict
    between Achilles and Agamemnon. It is clear that
    the two men have fought before, with Agamemnon
    having cheated Achilles of earlier prizes that
    he deserved, and Achilles having challenged
    Agamemnon's authority. A full-scale blow-out was
    inevitable given Agamemnon's low self-esteem
    (he does not really have the skill to control his

combined army) and Achilles' impulsiveness (he is
actually less than twenty years of age).

4.   Why exactly are these soldiers fighting? Why don't
     they just leave and go home?

> Though the war is purportedly being fought to
> win back Helen, whom Paris stole away from her
> husband Menelaus, the soldiers are ultimately there
> to win glory. They do this by accumulating meeds of
> honor—war prizes such as armor, gold, horses, and
> captive women like Chryseis and Briseis. When
> Agamemnon steals Briseis away from Achilles, he
> literally takes away some of Achilles' honor.

5.   Why is Agamemnon in charge of the combined army?

> Though one would expect Achilles to be the leader
> (because he is the strongest warrior) or perhaps
> Menelaus (since it was his wife Helen who was
> kidnapped by Paris), Agamemnon is chosen the
> leader because he has the most ships. This fact is
> made clear in the lengthy catalogue of ships that
> ends Book II. Agamemnon's job is not an easy one
> since he must command men who are themselves
> kings of their own city-states.

6.   Why is Achilles not immortal, since his mother is a
     goddess?

> Achilles is the son of the sea goddess Thetis and the
> mortal Peleus. In Greek mythology, one is immortal

only if both of his parents are gods. The situation is
made worse for Achilles, however, for he had been
destined to be the son of Thetis and Zeus. Zeus
had forced Thetis to marry a mortal because he
had heard a prophecy that Thetis would bear a son
who would be greater than his father. This knowledge, that he should have been immortal, increases
Achilles' obsession with death.

7. What are patronymics and epithets?

One of the clues that the *Iliad* began as an oral
poem is that there is a lot of repetition and padding
of poetic lines. As part of the oral tradition, all
major heroes had two kinds of tags attached to
their names: one was their patronymic (Greek for
"father's name"); the other was an epithet (a one or
two word adjective that captures some noble quality
of the soldier). Two examples in which both tags are
used would be: lordly Agamemnon, Son of Atreus;
swift-footed Achilles, son of Peleus.

8. What prevents Homer's soldiers from just taking whatever they want?

The *Iliad* takes place in a pre-law society. Order and
justice are maintained not by legal courts and police,
but by the careful instilling of virtues in the elite
members of society. All of Homer's soldiers, whether Greek or Trojan, have been taught from birth
to avoid shameful behavior (*aidos* in Greek) and
to not do anything that will bring blame (*nemesis*

in Greek) down upon them. When Achilles goes
berserk and shrugs off both *aidos* and *nemesis*, he
threatens the very foundations of his society.

9. Why does Hector leave the battlefield to enter the city
    of Troy in Book VI, and what happens to him there?

Hector returns temporarily to Troy for three
reasons: 1) to tell his mother Hecuba to pray to the
goddess Athena for aid; 2) to rouse up his brother
Paris to leave Helen's side and return to the battlefield; 3) to say farewell to his wife Andromache
since he knows he may not live much longer.
Significantly, all three women that he meets—his
mother, sister-in-law, and wife—try to prevent him
from returning to the war.

10. What is the relationship between Hector and Paris?

Hector clearly has a love-hate relationship with his
brother Paris. Though he accuses him of being a
coward, he nevertheless defends him and fights to
allow him to keep Helen. As with many sibling relationships, the older Hector is hurt when he hears
people ridicule his younger brother. He knows that
Paris is capable of courage and skill, but, being a
highly responsible and driven ("Type A") person, he
does not understand how Paris can be so cold and
indifferent to the soldiers who are suffering for him.

11. How does Homer depict Helen?

> Though Homer could easily have depicted Helen
> as a villainess, a brazen hussy who cares nothing for
> the men who are dying for her sake, he surprisingly
> presents a compassionate portrait of the woman
> who is the official cause of the Trojan War. It is not
> Homer, but Helen herself, who levels accusations
> against her. For Homer, Helen is merely a pawn in
> the petty squabbles of the gods.

12. Are Achilles and Patroclus gay?

> Nowhere in the *Iliad* is it even hinted that Achilles
> and Patroclus are gay lovers, despite the fond theo-
> ries of some critics. Although there is evidence that
> the tragic playwright Aeschylus wrote a play (now
> lost) in which the two are lovers, Homer does not
> present them as such. They are close friends, sharing
> a bond that many fellow soldiers share even today.
> Interestingly, Homer informs us that Patroclus is
> the elder of the two soldiers.

13. How does Homer depict the other Greek soldiers?

> Though Homer places the greater emphasis on
> Achilles and Agamemnon, he does take the time to
> develop other Greek soldiers: Aias (better known by
> his Latin name, Ajax) is presented as a pure soldier
> who seeks no help from the gods and prefers action
> to talking; Odysseus (Ulysses in Latin) is a smooth
> talker who uses his wits to help the Greeks in
> various ways; Diomedes is the most balanced of the

soldiers, knowing when to charge into battle and
when to hold back; Nestor is too old to fight himself but acts as a counselor to Agamemnon (and is a
reminder to all the soldiers that their fathers' gener-
ation was greater and stronger than their own).

14. Are Achilles' fellow soldiers mad at him for leaving the
war?

In the beginning, the soldiers are *not* mad at
Achilles for leaving the war, even though his
absence is causing many of them to die. They all
know that they are there for meeds of honor and so
sympathize with Achilles' anger over Agamemnon's
theft of his war prize. However, they warn him
that, if he does not accept Agamemnon's extremely
generous offer of meeds (including the return of
Briseis) and return, he will be in the wrong and will
bring *nemesis* down upon himself.

15. What does the presence of the gods add to the *Iliad*?

In addition to the things they do to drive forward
the plot, Homer's gods add a vital dimension to the
Iliad. Their immortality, which makes all of their
actions finally comic and even insignificant, brings
into sharp relief the tragic mortality of the soldiers,
particularly Achilles. As Book I begins with a quarrel between Achilles and Agamemnon, so it ends
with a quarrel between Zeus and Hera. However,
whereas the latter quarrel ends with laughter and
with Zeus and Hera retiring to their marital bed,

the former gives way to all the pain, terror, and
death of the *Iliad*.

16. Does Zeus simply predestine everything that happens
in the *Iliad*?

> Despite Zeus's power and wisdom, he does not
> stand above and outside fate. Oftentimes in the
> *Iliad*, his own plotting turns against him—as when
> his machinations lead to the death of his mortal
> son, Sarpedon. He weeps when Sarpedon dies but
> can do nothing to save him, even as he can do noth-
> ing to save Hector, whom he also loves and honors.
> For gods and men alike, choices have consequences.

17. Why does Homer spend so much time describing the
armor that Hephaestus makes for Achilles in Book
XVIII?

> Describing physical objects in detail is a device
> common to oral poetry; however, Homer uses
> Achilles' shield for far more than decorative purpos-
> es. On the shield, Homer has Hephaestus engrave
> two cities that represent the choice that all of us
> must make. In the one city a dispute, rather like the
> dispute between Achilles and Agamemnon, breaks
> out but is resolved by wise elders; in the other, a
> war, rather like the Trojan War, is being waged, but
> this conflict is inflamed by treachery and bloodlust.

18. Why does Homer devote all of Book XXIII to funeral
games for Patroclus?

Like the description of Achilles' shield, the inclusion of war games is an epic convention that allows for the inclusion of names and stories handed down by the oral tradition. Once again, however, Homer makes subtle and powerful use of it. First, by allowing us to watch the games, Homer shows us what war would be like if the soldiers were, like the gods, immortal. Alas, in our mortal world, the glory of combat brings death with it. Second, Homer climaxes the games with a chariot race in which an *Iliad*-like conflict almost breaks out between Menelaus (brother of Agamemnon) and Antilochus, the son of Nestor (a brave but impulsive young soldier like Achilles). The conflict, however, is resolved by Achilles himself, showing, as does the shield, that we can always choose the way of resolution.

19. What sad truth does Hector realize as he stands outside the walls of Troy in Book XXII and awaits the approach of Achilles?

As he watches the swift-footed Achilles bear down on him, Hector ponders things in his heart. He knows that he was foolish not to run inside the city walls as his father had begged him to do, but it is too late now. *What if,* he thinks to himself, *I were to surrender to Achilles and promise to give back Helen along with countless gifts?* Technically speaking, if Hector were to do that, the war would end and the Greeks would go home. But Hector realizes, in a moment of tragic enlightenment, that things have

gone too far for that. It is no longer about Helen.
As we proceed farther down the pathway of choice,
eventually we reach a point where we can longer
trace our way back.

20. How does Priam convince his wife Hecuba to allow
    him to sneak into the Greek camp to ransom back the
    body of their son from Achilles?

> In one of Homer's most beautiful and subtle literary
> moments, he has Priam offer to his wife, in Book
> XXIV, two of the same arguments that his son
> Hector offers to his wife Andromache in Book VI
> for why he must return to battle. First, Priam ex-
> plains that if he is fated to die, he will die, whether
> or not he enters the Greek camp. Second, he makes
> it clear that he would sooner die than see his city
> fall around him. Both father and son are like the
> proverbial captain who prefers to go down with his
> ship rather than outlive the crew for whose care he
> holds himself responsible.

21. What is Achilles' relationship to meeds of honor at the
    end of the *Iliad*?

> When the *Iliad* opens, Achilles is the poster boy
> for the meeds of honor system, but when Briseis
> is stolen from him, he pulls out of the war and
> cares nothing for prizes. When Patroclus dies, he
> does not return to the meeds of honor system, but
> decides that the only meed he desires is the death
> of Hector. After he grieves with Priam, however,

he subtly returns to the only system he knows, a change signaled by a moving scene in which he stands over the grave of Patroclus and apologizes for giving back Hector's body to Priam. Achilles knows Patroclus will forgive him, for, he explains to his dead friend, Priam gave him a noble ransom (meeds of honor), and he, Achilles, will share those prizes with him (by burning some of them on the funeral pyre).

FURTHER DISCUSSION AND REVIEW

Master what you have read by reviewing and integrating the five elements of this classic.

SETTING AND CHARACTERS

Be able to compare and contrast the personalities (including strengths, weaknesses, and mannerisms) of each character. How does the setting affect the characters?

PLOT

Be able to describe the beginning, middle, and end of the book along with specific details that move the plot forward and make it compelling. This includes the success or downfall (or both) of each character.

CONFLICT

Go through the character list and describe the tension between any and all main characters. Then, think about whether any characters have internal conflict (in their own minds). What is the significance of the overt conflict (fighting), or any conflict with impersonal forces?

THEMES

Be able to describe what this classic is telling us about the world. Is the message true? What truth can we take from the plot, characters, conflict, and themes (even if the author didn't believe that truth)? Do any objects take on added meaning because of repetition or their place in the story (i.e., do any objects become symbols)?

Be able to interact with and give examples for the following theme statements:

> The only way an individual can remain stable in the midst of great conflict and fear of death is by relying on a code or ethic that is greater than himself. In Hector's case, this is duty to his community; in Achilles' case, this is meeds of honor.

> The age-old tension between the leader, who must maintain law and order, and the charismatic loner, who has little regard for the rules, is aggravated by passion, fear, rage, and pride and is only calmed by self-moderation.

> Grief in response to mortality is the great human unifier; but peace, pity, and reconciliation in the presence of death can only come from an understanding of the intrinsic value of every human life.

Finally, compose your own theme statement about some element, large or small, of this classic. Then, use the Bible and common sense to assess the truth of that theme statement. Identify your own key words or borrow from the following list as a starting point: *mortality, war, honor, leadership, friendship, family relationships, fate and choice, grief, revenge, reconciliation.*

A NOTE FROM THE PUBLISHER:
TAKING THE CLASSICS QUIZ

Once you have finished the worldview guide, you can prepare for the end-of-book test. Each test will consist of a short-answer section on the book itself and the author, a short-answer section on plot and the narrative, and a long-answer essay section on worldview, conflict, and themes.

Each quiz, along with other helps, can be downloaded for free at www.canonpress.com/ClassicsQuizzes. If you have any questions about the quiz or its answers or the Worldview Guides in general, you can contact Canon Press at service@canonpress.com or 208.892.8074.

Dr. Louis Markos is a Professor of English and holds the Robert H. Ray Chair in Humanities at Houston Baptist University. He has written *From Achilles to Christ, Lewis Agonistes, Apologetics for the 21st Century, On the Shoulders of Hobbits,* and many other books on the classics and Victorian and Romantic prose and poetry. His articles have been published by *Christianity Today, Touchstone, Christian Research Journal,* and *Christian Scholar's Review,* among others, and his modern adaptations of Euripides' *Iphigenia in Tauris,* Euripides' *Helen,* and Sophocles' *Electra* have been performed off-Broadway. Lastly, he has also written a children's novel, *The Dreaming Stone,* in which his two kids become part of Greek mythology. In the sequel, *In the Shadow of Troy,* they become part of the *Iliad* and *Odyssey.*